Precarious

Precarious
Peter Raynard

Smokestack Books
1 Lake Terrace, Grewelthorpe, Ripon HG4 3BU
e-mail: info@smokestack-books.co.uk
www.smokestack-books.co.uk

ISBN 9780995767591

Smokestack Books
is represented
by Inpress Ltd

*'There comes a time when you realize that everything is a dream,
and only those things preserved in writing
have any possibility of being real.'*
James Salter

*To the memory of Michael Kennedy who told me I should write,
and Timmy Ryan who told me not to give a fuck.
I am still trying to learn both.*

Contents

Hello I am Peter and I have the name of my father   11
Missing memorials   12
When death ran in the family   13
Tic tacs at the track   14
Scholarship boys   15
The enquiries of an *inquieta adulescentia*   16
Red top nature watch   17
How to write the working classes   18
If we were real   20
Tommy and the common five-eighters   22
UK crews   24
Four white lads on their way to Black Uhuru, 1980   26
Our own personal Jesus   27
What's the good of legs if all you do is follow?   28
Now you're sucking diesel boy   29
Men made in his image   30
Empty mantelpieces   31
Seeing as he got away, let's do a Tarantino   32
Hands off Rosa Luxemburg   33
Marx versus God   34
The king with two shoes in his name   35
From a failed coast   36
The utility of tyres   37
A revolution in housing   38
God is an anarchist   39
The parliament of rot   41
Funding the troubles   42
Waiting on a rumour   43
Forget shedding for the wedding   44
Girls and boys come out to play   45
Different sharks, same waters   46
The slipping life   47
Psychosis at Orgreave   48
When the band didn't play on   49
They always come out fighting   50

Home education   51
Night watchman   53
Conversations with a son   54
Conversations with a dad   55
Coming off my meds listening to my son tic away   56
There are charities for all of my unequal parts   57
Coming off my meds when you are all asleep   60
Sertraline earworms   61
How to keep the little beggars quiet   62
For Tommy it's all about the music   63
Man up man down   66
For most men it goes without saying   67
Veteran   70
A US soldier after Belshazzar's Feast   71
A lesson in extreme sports for the untrained soldier 72
Lunchtime   73
He was a man of many words   74
The case of the quiet caretaker   75
Colluding with the enemy   77
Our lost history   78
Meat down the cally   79
This isn't a party, my friend   81
Testosterone injection   82
Chatting up the barmaid   83
We are none of us Sisyphus   84
A classical 4-4-2 formation   85
Ezekiel's burden   86
It's not a matter of life and death, but still   87
Bored to death   88
If you don't go to theirs, they won't go to yours   89
In the words of st peter   90
Is it writing or is it typing?   91
How to avoid poetry   93

Hello I am Peter and I have the name of my father

Before you were thought of, conceived, or born,
as the first boy, your name was given to you
by your father's faith; handed down
like a broken watch or faded picture of long forgotten
ancestors hiding in a bottom drawer.

Carrying this weight of two names
to be passed on, you went out, to find a wife
and bear a son, since that was the way
to honour men. Look, there's old Peter
with his son Pete, and Thomas with Tommy;
today they've got their own millennium boys,

Isaac, Felix, Xavier and Jacob, rewriting
their granddads' line in the sand,
as the old men spin above their graves
asking: who will name their world now?

Missing memorials

We hear them coming for us
in our sleep. Stamping the stairs
out of silence. Standing
over us, their jaws
a slaver of laughter. We piss
ourselves, sensing the fading
boredom of their shift. They take photos
with their fists leave us
like two slides of unreliable evidence.
We say we get it. We promise.
Quiet as a fingerprint, we listen
to our bones and history, broken
into neat paper columns
of Births, Marriages, Deaths.

When death ran in the family

My gran pushed out my mother into a stable
of siblings the last of ten, in times when

succession was a given. The same day, in another ward,
her twelve year old brother was taken away by TB.

Five survived their childhood days, the rest never
passed the test that lay behind local school gates.

My mother lost her father when she was three
a stolen memory in an age of incessant grief.
Gran took it all on, through the war in the face

of an absent state, fighting for every child's breath.
She went on to own two tellies, broken but still

with their use, '*one's for ITV, one's for BBC*',
without betraying her roots. Trying to keep up

with history, it took a generation to turn grey before
infant deaths no longer ran in the family round our way.

Tic tacs at the track

They stood out beaconed on their boxes.
I could only see them from the shoulder up:
White gloves weaving those magic odds
out the ear, *top of the head*, or *on the nose*.

Punters would follow their semaphore to see
an *Up-the-arm*, an *Ear'ole*, or a *Major Stevens*
flying overhead. Dad joked they were sending
messages to the deaf. The odd time a *Double Carpet*

flew past the line by a short head, the bookies
cracked a smile, plus the punter whose pin
had pricked the right spot for once. The serious
men, long coated with cigars in hand, strode
up with *bags of sand* to take on a *short one*;

if it wasn't *odds on* it'd be *straight up*,
a *shoulder* maybe, a *bottle* max. I'd watch them
walk back like cons, pick out their bins and scan
the track like Churchill overseeing the troops.

My old man had less money but no less sense.
He often lost me amongst the legs when putting
on his bet, laying a *sky diver* or *cock and hen* – lowest
he took was *top-of-the-head*, *carpet*, or *Burlington Bertie*,

up to a *cockle*. If a top jockey was on a *macaroni*
he'd drop a couple on. Each way he wasn't going to win
enough for a long coat. He always tried to leave though
with a cigar, blowing smoke all the way home.

Scholarship boys

Unlucky enough to pass our eleven plus
we were claw-crane selections
from our class dropped into a history
the likes of us had never read.

Inducted with pictured corridors
of Spiritus Vicis spouting opportunity
from the mothballed grammar
of the cloak-wielding Headmaster
and his fountain of Latin characters.

Amo, amas, a matter of opinion
was to know our place. Our mouths
were swabbed for memories.
We were to become
someone else's nostalgia.

By the time we left early,
five of a seven-year stretch,
we stooped off to the factories
that laughed at us
for taking the long way round.

The enquiries of an *inquieta adulescentia*

Is it done by you? For you? To you? Lying,
sitting, standing, in/out shaking like
a trout? Is it meant to be hard
or easy? Is it a thrill, a drill, a well-oiled
spill? What about the leftovers? Wrapped,
flushed, forgotten? A daily exertion?
When do you know you want another go?
Can people tell if you've just done it?
If so, then who would they tell? Is it a sin
like pride? What about the boy, the washing
up glove and a gap in the mattress? Is that
a joke? What about the boy shouting
down to his mum in distress at the mess
made from an alien urge? Where's best
to hide the mag you stole from your dad,
your mum's catalogue, page after page
of Internet history, you can delete for free?
Is such pleasure meant to have that look?
Does it always make that noise? Will you
take me by the hand when I'm done?

Red top nature watch

(a message from the paper's editor)

An exhausted sun blisters its last
through the estates. Framed on balconies,
people glow in the end of day heat.
Foil tray barbecues watch bottles of beer
oscillate at forty-five degrees per minute
to a cacophony of fairground-heavy soundtracks.
This is the grace of their nature.

Sirens climb to compete with
a car horn's impatience, where voices
float into friendly debate. Bare ribbed kids
let loose on dusty playgrounds
dizzy with the fizzy they kick a ball
through an escape in the fence
they will never future through.

Police, insurgents in hostile air space
disturb the self-induced serenity
of social tenancy. Retarding back
to their sugar white tea break,
leaden with spreadsheets of performance
that tie their hands, in a neat bow.

The crest of this summer's day
on its descent to a dandruff night sky,
is lit by these people, like stars yet to present.
But keep looking, something will go wrong.
It always does. It's where all good stories come from.

How to write the working classes

(e-mail from the paper's editor)

For your purposes, the collective noun for the working class is 'These People' or 'Those People' never 'The People' or 'My People'. Ideally you are looking for an inbred, saggy clothed, Sports Direct, Union Jack pale-faced male who claims he can trace his ancestors back to Neanderthal times. They'll have a tight-leashed muscle-bound dog, with rabid flecked jaw, ravenous for an outsider's hairy calf.

The female of the species, will be a barely been to school, heavily made up heavily pregnant, ciggie hanging from botoxed-lipped slag with a neck tattoo of an ex-boyfriend, pushing a brown skinned baby wailing its lungs out. Bonus if she's got slightly older multi-coloured offspring biting at her heels.

For interviews, go to a rainy Saturday market where salt-of-the-earth traders shout *'cum an' 'av a look, pand a bowl'* & other such unintelligible tongue-juggling noises, to try and get you to buy their rotting fruit and veg. Swear about the weather, then ask *'how's business gavna?'* before moving on to *'do you think there are too many immigrants living in your back garden?'* or *'how would you feel if your daughter came aboard with a Caribbean rapper?'*

When describing their estate, use words like concrete, boarded up, brutal, dank, bleak, unloved – pepper your sentences like a rancid Berni Inn steak. Get them to heap blame on the metropolitan elites, who they feel rule over them like hand-me-down warlords from Henry the VIII; politicians will be the main target, but they'll also harp on about big business, the council, estate agents, & middle-class teachers who make their kids learn German or Jihadi.

Talk of Brexit will give vent to their alleyway of opinions on independence, from '*now we can take our country back*' to '*now we can send them all back*'. (Btw, only ever mention the Royal Family, when getting them nostalgic). Pretend to take copious notes to induce a feeling they're finally being listened to. Don't waste time on their cultural interests, you'll only get them gabbing on about their second hand cousin removed who got to the regional semi-finals of *Britain's Got Talent* with their rendition of *God Save the Queen* whistled entirely through their left nostril (the other one will have a ring through it).

If they start talking about pigeons or their collection of dominoes trophies, close them down, as you'll end up in some mouldy old shed, offered a roll up and a mug of quarried tea. When you leave, slip them a score (that's a twenty) tell them it's been real, then rush off home to submit copy, neck a whisky, snort a line then shower yourself furiously, as if you've just been raped.

If we were real

Jo's mum Helen is a slag,
doesn't stop her having a go
at Jo getting pregnant by a black man
and staying in a hole
with that pansified little creep though.

Colin's mum is no better,
she's just after his dead dad's
insurance money, but Colin's
a little toe rag running for his life,

who'll let the whole fucking lot
of them down. Arthur's a proper
hard bastard, working his seed
into as many women as he can.

And guess what, Victor's only gone
and got his missus up the ready rough,
so has to live with the mother-in-law,
and she's had a leading role

in working men's jokes for years.
Tommy's off up the match, an away game
kick-the-shit out of any proper casual
who'll have it. Ray beats up his missus
when he gets home, stamps on her throat

like some rat he found in the bog. Lol's Dad
commits the horrors with her sister
and her mate any place he can, then tries
it on with her until Combo ends the cunt.

Young Timmy knows how to enjoy himself,
he cleans double breasted windows,
or checks under the sink for some
scantily clad plumbing, before delivering

a whipped cream double entendre
to bored housewives. Rita likes a bit
of that an' all, off shagging Bob,
with her mate Sue, but her namesake

tries her hand at books instead of dotting
her luck on the bingo of a Saturday night.
Shirley's fucked off to Greece, can't stand
talking to the wall no more, cooking

egg 'n chips for her husband,
who believes that's a woman's place.
Billy's dad knows what a man should be,
and it's not a fucking dancer.

Rent's smacked off his boat, so goes swimming
for a pearl in the filth of the bog,
whilst Dushane's a boy at the top
of his game, on the estates round his way.

Like Frank's kids, who surround him
like a wreath, this all may be true.
And Big Chris is right when he says,
'It's been emotional.'
But is that really all we are?
Do we not go by any other names?

Tommy and the common five-eighters

SOME OF US are washer-women wet-nurse birth mothers of a nation of shopkeepers, fitters and lifters. Smothered suffragettes stuffed down the back of the Pankhursts' sofa.

SOME OF US are trench-foot perfect-fit coffin fodder taken in by the pointed finger of men bred from a moustache to dig a scar down France to bury ourselves in.

SOME OF US march from Jarrow for the jobs of those who survive with hats and caps in hands, dead men who fell again in Spain, then one year on return as common five-eighters in uniform size to beat the Germans second time around, then on to Seoul, to Suez, to Aden and a British flag gravestone memorial with an empty can of Stella & a vodka miniature salute to Afghanistan, Iraq, & Woolwich.

SOME OF US are Mothers Against Murder and Aggression, against a change in benefits, for a change in child support from Fathers for Justice, for families without two-up two-down parents, where there is fighting in the pockets of lawyers and the social.

SOME OF US work black hole hours in pits, on sites, warehouses and factories doing much more work than eight hours a day. A weakling won't last long before becoming your average Joe, man on the street, freezing fucking cold over a brazier, with rolled up fingers watching scabs' shadows pass through bus windows.

SOME OF US get stuck into the middle.

SOME OF US are pork-pie pasty-faced full English no time for breakfasts, cash-in-handover fist with no questions asked just singing knees up Mother Brown's sweet and sour bingo wings, doing the Lambeth Walk-the-talk in training sessions with benefit lessons screened on CCTV for viewing by fat twats in stained ties.

SOME OF US are a backdraft rush of colonial need, blown in from the shanties and fields, away from the famine, war *and* poverty, to plant seeds on the buses, wards, and shop corners of peoples' minds.

SOME OF US come from a different kind of estate, born in a crib that turns graves' end, out east where the pearls of history garnish clothes&caps and our favourite philosopher is *Kant.*

SOME OF US are Grunswick, Orgreave, Tottenham, Toxteth, Brixton, made in Dagenham, the horror stories and fairy tales of brass bands, ballet dancers, strippers and trainspotters, loan sharks with borstal knuckles dotted ACAB, that can't be a rhyme scheme & I'm the Daddy now, cunt.

SOME OF US are blue collared *what time do you call this? Dinner's in the doghouse!* with a belly like a party seven, and lungs defunct as an all-out strike. We turn white collar for Sunday Mass, the blood of Christ, the pub, a crisp burnt roast, slippers and a kip, then a string vest costume drama in front of a three bar fire.

Then it's Monday and work, & there's Tommy, head as heavy as an elephant's coffin, choking for a smoke and a trap to empty himself in. He just thanks fuck he's still got Page 3, that page at the start of a book he can read in the bog in peace, as the intestines of industry grind away inside him.

UK crews

(after Kyle Dargan)

Those train carriage
boys. Those
away game boys.
Those simple
inner-city shire boys.
Those terrace end
boys. After one
another's colours boys.
Those stab-and-slash
Mothered boys, in
their feathered footsteps.
Chants claim grounds,
hunters gather, mind
your language boys.
Keep fighting
on barren ground
where you meet
your match boys.

But what of those
other boys?
Those Apple-eyed
boys, screen saver
faces, hedging,
laying bets to offset
debts boys.
Pin-striped
laugh-line boys.
Watch those boys
eating up the Southeast
square mile
meals paid on receipt

by others boys.
Open-legged,
cocksure slug,
go figure boys.

See all those boys?
At whose violence
do we lay ourselves
open to now boys?

Four white lads on their way to Black Uhuru, 1980

And we are marching, rising up with borderless rhythm, genetically mixed beats, Far I growling, Upsetters cheering, Head Charge chanting, stepping

from our skin, uniting the left and right side of our brains. Heeding a four/four beat, smooth as Night Nurse or the guy who sold us cheap weed

with fire-cracking seeds that burn our nose. The money's signed on for, the van siphoned to the max, we spark a spliff careful not to catch a fire

with our petrol lips. Late as a dealer we drive to Shakespeare bass upon Dunbar snares along the M45 out of Coventry. Shooting past Babylon

leaving a cloud of collie on the outside lane, they light up under blue sirens. We are burned. The coming decade is a road of hot coals and we can't dance.

Our own personal Jesus

With scrag-rust hair blessing coat hanger shoulders,
an errant beard nesting on his chest, he scare-crowed kids
who scuttled behind their mothers. Walked with a dirty
old man raincoat covering a bone tight frame. Kept it
closed most year round with special opening hours
to pocket a bottle of Thunderbird only the brave
said came from a grape. His promiscuous choice
of fag ends coloured his nails autumn.

An out-of-the bluecoat Englishman amongst a bog
of tricolour boys, they welcomed him with the palsied
humour of a cul-de-sac. Regaled tales of a mother's ruin
on the pub car park stage, a sage that turned us into
a front row firing squad of laughter at a joke that wasn't told.
Thrown coins saw him shadow off for another bottle
putting in city miles for hours with no end. A patrol car
on the border of sanity, a charge sheet no-one could read.

At the finish line his no show drew blanks, leaving
an invisible mark. Unearthed at home amongst
books and his daily scatter of scrawls papering
the floor; found words unread that turned out
to be streets ahead of theirs or mine.

What's the good of legs if all you do is follow?

A Pioneer with a sweep of grey hair laid bare by the wind,
your father stands askance of the pitch each week. Once a farmer
with a tenor's chest he was born to call the moiled cows at the fleeting
dusk. He curses you through cupped hands hard as a donkey's hooves
each time you pass the ball square or a player puts you on your arse.

Too good for your own good, you were born to go up front
with older lads who bound around in shirts that honour hours
spent puffing up their cushions in the gym. You are drawn by
the tails of them at the depths of their powers into bars for a few
women more, or more likely the round of a table smoking with stories
about touchlines of old men losing their voices and their own sight of goal.

Now you're sucking diesel boy

A four o'clock Saturday cattle market overspill
of bets laid in a script on the counter,
like ancient religious scrawls. Some shout
for you to write their fortune – *'you've lucky
handwriting so you have'*. Win or lose, at
race end they slide the slip back under
the glass, like used bog roll. *'Not this time Sean,
I'm afraid.' 'Will ya not write me out a winner
next time?' 'Only if I can write your will as well.'*
Everyone hates the English when it comes
to sport. Football's the bone they gnaw on
Brady or Bonner, George Best, though he came
from the other side of the North. Cricket is for old
colonial types & no-one bets on the hurling.

Church is a totem routine, as much as tradition,
come Sunday morning. Trails of dark suits,
blue dresses, kids with slick grease hair in shirts
whiter than the Priest's teeth against his collar,
or the head of an old man's pint as it yellows
at the bottom. Round the back, teenage dreamers
with fag ash tashes, still afraid of their mam's beliefs,
smoke into life, sending a short straw in to see
who's giving Mass. *'Was it Father Cafferty
or Father Coughlan?' 'Cafferty, mam.'*
'Good lad.' She already knew the answer.
Streets fill, empty, fill until the end of a day
stained in prayers, holy communion, the Lord's
gateway drug to the pub or club; all the passing
of another week you've no mind to rewind
in case you remember who you are, who you'll be,
or who emptied your pocket of all its luck.

Men made in his image

We screamed at the Priest during our church baptism,
as though burned by the future of holy water.
Thank God my father left the clutch of such tradition
saving me from false confirmation. At the altar,

this fiend, ruined the young voices of a captured choir
and church football team. Towel dry boys were watched as
they changed, picking out special ones on the quiet.
I shared fags with some of them outside Sunday Mass,

as his sermon branded creed into families' beliefs.
Where I could go home, they were forced to confess
fake sins to him on a bent faith, only to receive
foul penance in the tombs of their mouths. He left

before a few boys – now men – went on and shared
a life where children were neither seen nor heard.

Empty mantelpieces

Here,
he christened, confirmed, married, and buried.
Placing God's moon on a trust of tongues.
Handing down rituals like old clothes,
he catechised clichés of Heaven and Hell
bringing the old country with him,
to a new place prayed and paid for.

Here,
he abused his charisma, his charm.
He was a pickpocket, a mass magician;
stole the innocence of the '*there-there*' boys,
conjured a congregation of silence, victims all,
though no-one spoke.

Here,
it was all caught on camera,
Christenings, Confirmations, weddings,
a gallery of shouldered smiles.
Only the dead were exempt.
Pictures of distant days printed
in black and white joy, now blurred
in a jaded hush, are days they can look at
no more. Locked away like their voices.

There is nothing left to see
across the fireplaces of the last century.

Seeing as he got away, let's do a Tarantino

Let's smash all of the empties, stamp them back to sand,
build castles in the car park, line turrets with flaming flags.

Let's build a fuck-off tank, roll it over to the church,
lay siege upon his holiness, watch him fucking squirm.

We'll eat all of his Sunday meat, chew him till he's raw,
miscarriage red at the altar we'll steal all of the chords

from the organ, tie him up in the Lord's Prayer,
Hail Mary the aisle with bullets sprayed across the floor.

We'll lie that we forgive him, as he did unto us,
promise to watch over him, but then we'll fucking cross

him. We'll stand him up taut, so he can see us turn,
then set fire to his cassock, watch the fucker burn.

Hands off Rosa Luxemburg

'Red Rosa now has vanished too… She told the poor what life is about, And so the rich have rubbed her out. May she rest in peace.'
Bertolt Brecht

Red Rosa was carved from timber
in a Poland that was not her own.
She was not '*mistaken, mistaken, mistaken*',
dear Lenin. Your *eagle of the working classes*
hawked a different path never landing
on another's arm. She was Spartacus,
who kept moving to hear her chains,
advancement through struggle, the true manifesto.

She could smell the stinking corpse of Germany
at a time when people held their nose. Called the workers
to revolt as gravediggers of the state, to lay down
their tools and take arms not against a common
class in some Great War they didn't own.

Rising up she took the butt and bullet of a rifle
to her head, her hands and ankles wired,
severed like her struggle but not her history.
Her country was a flag she never raised, her blood
without borders flowed into the river she was flung.

'*Freedom is always the freedom of the dissenter*';
it does not rest, not in peace, but within
the: '*I was, I am, I will be!*'

Marx versus God

I've seen all the poster boys of communism;
Marx & Engels, Lenin & Trotsky, Guevara & Castro.
Read each of them all, an all, an all, like torn out
pages of porn found down the fields. Plastered

them up in a book of scrap kept under the bed. Watched
endless clippets of their icon-you-not speeches,
unfurled egos from the throats of Mao to Chavez.
Agreed with a lot of the wind, caught up in their sails

flapping like a butterfly's wing. Saw them cult-like,
occupy the minds of disciples stood outside High Street
brands flashing indoctrination with no gloss but full
of emulsion to slip between the arse-cheek IQs of passers-by.

I'm from those masses, full of coke and free of opium,
watching Kentucky fried mind-fattening programmes
where the runt of personality is wrapped up like bikini-clad
mags written by middle class lads you buy on your way

to the tills, along with breath fresh mints and full strength
condoms. I've been in the pubs & clubs, shop floors & sites,
school gates & libraries. Been on protests & marches,
took part in witch hunts of rich cunts we never managed

to kick the fuck out of. I've been with all of those comrades,
holding kids & sickles, books & shovels, remotes and Molotovs.
But I never could decide whether to stick with the pack or twist
my arms back and let them hang, broken by my side, as God
intended.

The king with two shoes in his name

At the dawn of the Scramble, the King of Lesotho lies dead.
I am in the presence of his lineage, drinking too quickly
in a single bulb room in Pretoria. The resistance brewed
here less than ten years from where I sit; it is still seen
in the faces of men, served by Shebeen Queens.
'*You spell my name with two shoes – Moshoeshoe,*'
he jokes, but there is a razor at the throat of history
when pronouncing it: '*Moshwayshway*', the sound
made by the King, as he shaved the beards
of his enemies in death-conquering raids;
the silver swish of victory. The King lost
his seeds to Dutch & British bullets 'civilising'
the continent, leaving but a tenth that Africans
could call their own by the Great War's end.
He takes me to Soweto, to a small home. I feel
whiter than Rhodes, but he insists. Tea is served
then quietly on leaving, money is given to our host.
It is the township's permanence that strikes,
development is elastic, a contested deceit.
The land is said to be theirs now, but not the fruits
of their seed. Soweto and Lesotho are dry islands;
Kings & Queens remain – they are drowning with thirst.

From a failed coast

There, for someone's reason, someone's gain.
Against surging great gulps of salt and scars
of a slave grave sky, your mother tongue. It is
there to escort you, to save you, to end you
over and over again by its traffic of tides
that never move to a part-time moon.

Squat tight, fold your frame into bowed beams
formed against their will, feel it mould
your fate. A rhythm not tamed by self-control.
Listen as it tears sheets from the storm,
slashes them under, giving rise to horizons of wars
that never cease, and a death they call thunder.

The utility of tyres

O! We know how you roll. We pushed you down
dew-licked hills skittling spittle-tongued livestock,
shooting off to the farmer's double barrel salute.

More present than God, from Lego to Monster Trucks –
size matters for boy racer skid marks, in a perfect
day trip to Margate or bank job getaway.

But for others O how you burn. Here, flames blow
smoke rings on blocked roads, choking for control
from Belfast to Beirut. Over there you are no match

for the shock of bombs. So you are put to good use
around the necks of men, from Haiti to the Cape. Laced
in petrol, a spark sears a collaborator's skin taking away

any trace of him. You? You lose shape, a closed eye,
as people drive by knowing there is nothing left to see.

A revolution in housing

Arise   you high-rise   arise
end slumming-it and rent-to-kill
take flight you council cathedrals
attack the sham mammon of steel

Ring out your bells with the cry
we have no fear of defeat
take every slice of the sky
make treason of the streets

Occupy! Occupy Royal Parks
Richmond Greenwich, have belief
seat your castles atop Crystal Palace
Highgate & Hampstead Heath

Take another view, cause trouble,
remember the Putney Debates
don't give in to the lies of rubble
gift new meaning to the estates

Across the romance of capital
London has muckles of space
dream away constructions so brutal
as you sleep by ponds and lakes

No more the square miles of money
will feast on delights such as us
their wealth kills all that is worthy
lest we forget all those we have lost.

God is an anarchist

They handcuff their earrings
                                        to the naked landlords' wrists
Papier-mâché tenancy agreements
                                        leave a lipstick kiss

They steal politicians from their slumber
                                        who shape laws as they breed
They were found down the market
                                        where they learned to breathe

They party with professors
                                        steal their footnotes masked as facts
Graffiti phlegm-lined symbols
                                        tagged like Ancient Maths

They re-designed the architects,
                                        drew them with a spliff
hung them from their high rise minds,
                                        then kicked them off a cliff

They sell prophesies to Priests
                                        conning a free passage to the past
The clerics are meant for the long haul
                                        but their prayers never last

They killed the Royal Families
                                        lopped off all their heads
crowns without a title
                                        they were murdered in their beds

The Gods send down their angels
                                        to see what's going on
They are all at the Beltane
                                        riding on white swans

The angels return with smiles
                        tell the Gods that all is fine
The Gods thank God at such good news
                    and go on to neck more wine.

The parliament of rot

Maybe if we listen to the land
flouting all that was taught us,
we can rout the certainty
we were born into. For within
this infinity of tiny deaths
there is a song we are instilled from.

Maybe if we believe
that fires ember beneath
our fingernails, we can scratch
the face off this country. I tell you
within its bones is fated
a painting so ulcerous
it should never have been hung.

Funding the troubles

They collected on a regular occasion
like ghosts recruiting for the dead
soldiers on British soil without a gun
you drank your pint and dared not lift your head

until you put a hand into your pocket
hoping still to find some coins leftover
as change would have rattled the bucket
but palming notes meant you went home sober.

One lad didn't know what was happening
broke a silence that betrayed his fear
a tool well beyond the sharpening –
new recruits never could hold their beer.

None of us became brothers in that band.
Fuck, we'd only just broke free of our mams.

Waiting on a rumour

A bag of wind blows in with a breathless
'they're coming to take the pub', ah ha,
'they're coming to take the pub,' all over

a no mark's arm, broken with a pool cue
we had no part in. *'They can fucking take it –*
the beer's shit,' says one.*'It was my cue'*,

replies an eight ball clearance. Brothers,
cousins, other numb-nut graduates
from the same terraces, were gathering

in the minds of us nervous pints, staring
at the pool table, like gatecrashers at a wake.
Sticky as a girlfriend beyond our reach, the piss-

patterned carpet keeps us in our seats. A cunt's
a cunt for all that but a lad's six-month sling,
doesn't require a rogues' reunion. We're a quiver

of livers in the prisoners' dilemma of being
either battened down by inbreeds, or by each other?
Easy, for there's really no need to come and spoil

such a perfectly carved night, we are not titans, we can fuck
ourselves up, when our minds are left to their own devices.

Forget shedding for the wedding

Our grans stuck two fingers up to Churchill
now we are a free bird brood of dayglow
spandex, pink cheeked shrink-wrapped like a no frills
condom. Loud as a pair of slapped thighs, blow

your ears out they could if you got lucky.
No care for long term health plans, guaranteed
by a wank-worn salesmen's signature. We've
smiles as wide as our Mum's 1960s

C-section. Long left our seed-free coitus
back of the bus singing karaoke
covers of *'fuck you we won't do as you
tell us,'* cock wipe. Cos we know every

song of innocence, so leave well alone
we are the bitches and we've got the bone.

Girls and boys come out to play

They have an orchard of cider,
scrumped up inside them.
A back room frontload ritual,
helps take on a clusterfuck
of men with shirt-tailed tongues
lapping up their short skirt shores.

These girls are bright as fluorescent
strip lights, experts in the jab and weave
of a lad's patter – they flicker the needy,
greedy, semen-eyed mum fluffs,
sprayed in eau-to-moan
glow-in-the-dark tumescence-
experts – ha! – in ten ways to *'bag a slag'*.

Boys dripping under their own
pressure of go and get them
if you think you're hard enough
to splay a purse; limp dicks
with nerves of dysentery, rush
to the bog for lines of Charlie,
taken from a Grand Theft Autocue,
fingered under sticky sheets.

Boys who drop chat up lines
in a girl's drink; hoping she'll swallow
every fizz & flavour, trying to shatter
a *Dog Star* sparkling in a chandelier.
But these girls still know how to shine.

Different sharks, same waters

We are a high street of sweaty arses
with interest free Lexus-driven ambition.

Can't keep up with your payments?
We've got a knack for that/an app for that,
with an ambivalent account toward risk glee debt.

No family is left behind. Got a passion
to perform, let us give you extra,
we're fluid in finance, offer protection,

a greed apart. Cash if you die, cash
if you don't, we put people into homes.
The right relationship is everything.

Step up make it happen – if there's a corner
we're around it. It's time to wake up to life!

*

This one is a shadow of a morning
at the stainglass council door
that opens to his force over

and over again. Feel the rough
of his chin at her neck, the fear
of the last debt on his breath,

hands medium rare round her waist,
with a bulging wad. Pushing back she
sees the loss-making terms & conditions

of a moneyed fist. An under-song
of zero hour pay making it impossible
to return all that she doesn't owe.

The slipping life

Hospital lights never flatter the sick
and I have a Priest at my feet, stroking
the soles with fingers as thick as candles;
rubbing away he is, crossing skin as thin
as parchment. I hope he won't speak
for I've not the strength to tell him
there's no need for his words, never was.
Just keep rubbing those feet Father
I want to say, for it takes me away
from barren glands and bones angling
their escape from a sixteen-year-old
failing inside a five-stone frame.

My mother is a machine of worry
rocking away in the corner, knitting
a story she hopes won't need telling.
My doctor strides in loaded with science,
sufferance, and diagnoses. Our Father
gives me a knowing look. Hearing the news,
my mother, all bible and ancestry jumps up,
'*Ah Father, it's a miracle!*' and kisses
a lifetime of faith on the hand of a man
with all the luck of the devil. The doctor
lays a warm hand on my head, slips away
to the banality of sheet white certainty.

Psychosis at Orgreave

The miners are climbing the walls
of the TV room. Shadows of men,
striking against the psyche ward's
bleach streaked floors. I must have
come in late as short-shielded police
are at them, a royal force of nature
captured by Thatcher's hook. I'm in
my dressing gown off my fucking nut.
I sit on that piss-resistant chair
with a rip in it, watching the circus.

For days I've been stared at by faces
in the paper, shadows in the corner
chatting about me as I eat cereal;
my old man tells me they're not there,
I don't believe him. Just ignore them
then, he says. I laugh milk from my nose
at that. The psyches come at me
with their questions, none of which make sense.

I'm up for the battle to go on, to see it
spread beyond boot dust fields, away
from the shiny lino and sleep filled wards.
I turn to the telly for reality, they are there,
an infantry in blue, running, chasing, hunting,
clubbing; the filth don't give a fuck, it's all
spinning. That's enough for me. I'm away.

I wake, to wet and warm between my legs.
A low paid Florence kneels at my lap,
the psyche in waiting at her shoulder.
Questions come at me, a medical catechism
I've learned the answers to. They finally ask,
'Do helicopters eat their young?' I reply,
'Yes, yes they do. I just saw them, over there.'

When the band didn't play on

You know that band? What they called?
The band that gave you permission;
the band that blew the bloody doors off.
Who stood you upright, against the face
of X & Y cardboard chromosomes, dressed
as show homes on streets lined with every sign
except a U-turn. The band that took you away
like a rapture cult. Yes, that's the band.

Side B

He loved a band like that. Too much too young
for a tattoo of them, he taped their name
on his stomach and lay out in the sun.
Loud as a speaker when he ripped off
the tape to bear a tan surrounding
their name, the summer he turned sixteen.
When the leaves turned crisp as his skin,
the band's name remained; he began
to brown at the elbows & knees, his eyes
were in retreat. By Christmas, he was
a rack of ribs with the band's name
disfigured across the bowl of his belly.
Until finally, there was nothing left
but a map of him on the bed sheets
in a silent ward no parent wants to listen to.

They always come out fighting

Blue-masked anaesthetists joke about
a colleague's fate, as our son crowns

his entrance, forceps clamped around
a half-born head to coerce an escape.

But he is stubborn, more stubborn than
the surgeon who resigns him back

inside his exhausted mother. A colleague
is to be sacked, for a habit of absence, as

our son is to be cut out like a car crash.
A clear mask is put over my wife's face,

held there by a man as if filling up his motor.
Blue tarpaulin is erected below her breasts,

she is to become an open wound. They squirt
water over her ribs, ask if can she feel anything.

Tracing the surgeon's slice, I want to be put
under. One mask asks another *anything good*

on the telly tonight, as I am drawn by a display
of lights glowing red with the pipes and organs

of her insides, announcing a son reaching up
out of his mother to screech his entrance;

a bloodied pugilist with fists clenched,
exposing us all to unending rounds of worry.

Home education

The sound of heavy metal urges us on
as I take my son to school for an exam.
Wipers thrash away at the hail, whilst I try
translating the road. Stopping for lights,

he turns off the music, looks at the side
of my face, tells me *he's been feeling down
lately, getting into trouble, bunking off
school, it's all become too much.*

The lights go green, he rolls up
his right sleeve, says he is *sorry.*
My left eye is a better judge than
my right, so between ninety-degree

flicks of the head, I try to decipher
a Morse code of dashes from wrist
to elbow on his left arm. Driving
toward a landmark of questions,

a scroll of rain unfurls before me,
severing all major routes to the future.

*

Back home his mind breaks into kindling; it's time
to listen to his music, watch his videos, drink with him,
smoke with him, play GTA with him – to talk, over
and over, sifting words to find a way he will stay.

The sight of his arm makes me think of harming
myself, to share another's pain. The shirts I buy
him are now all long-sleeved. I know where he is
taken in his sleep, how his image hangs on the wall

and its face chants: '*Do it, do it.*' He talks about
the worst way to end one self – '*hanging in the woods
is an emo cliché & pills are too easy*'. I pray he won't
give in to impulse, knowing it is not a selfish act. So,
I top up my lungs, but I dare not yet breathe out.

Night watchman

Bed by midnight, I set my alarm for two a.m.
At its sound I pad to my son's room.   The floor
is a rubble of clothes, guitar leads, a trophy cabinet
of sticky bowls residue in a corner.

        In bed, he holds the glow of his screen,
perched in fear of the grave hymns that sing
in his dreams.   He says he's okay, without shifting.
I fail by saying '*try to get some sleep*'.

        I retreat to my bed, risk an hour.
At three he's still glowing. Says he tried.
I know.   Best rise for a time.

I wipe last night's words from the kitchen table.
We eat cereal to silence, see if that works.
It's being tested with everything else outside
the covers of a book.   Back in bed,

he turns to the wall.   Now I stay, see him to sleep.
At the inhale of day, the sun cracks its knuckles
behind the curtains.   '*Come on then*,' I say.

Conversations with a son

Get up. It's two o'clock. In the afternoon! Did you sleep okay?
Do you want something to eat? You'll turn into a noodle.
Have a shower while I make them. Clean your nails.
Tidy your room.You put new strings on? That's good.
When did you learn that? That's brilliant. Play it again.
Reminds me of Sabbath. Can I wear your Hendrix top? No,
you can't borrow my undies. Don't eat too fast. You did what?
You're kidding me? What do you say to them? I'd slap 'em.
Watch yourself. Where you been? Who with? You eaten?
Do you want a beer? Cheers. You've already got two piercings.
Thank God, for the law on tattoos. No, I never took smack.
What about that lad at your school? Did you know him?
How'd he do it? Fucking hell. Day before exams, as well.
What did your psyche say? About looking after yourself?
Don't worry about it. I know, original. Relax.
Try to keep calm. Breathe. Are you alright now?
You must be tired. Go to bed then. Don't play your music.
Turn off your light. Go to sleep it's two o'clock.
Goodnight son.

Conversations with a dad

mornin' two o'clock? what? i'll get up in a minute
took ages to get to sleep i'm bare hungry can I have noodles?
I'll have a shower tomorrow it's tidy can you bleach my roots?
these jeans were clean on last week
listen to this me, just made it up you kidding me?
this is hard-core, duh! you heard the new Cancer Bats album?
i took mushrooms once i drank bong water once sick as a dog
I often get called a faggot I don't say anything to 'em
dun't bother me can't fight them all
outside youthy with the lads nah, not hungry
hobgoblin? go on then cheers
can I get my lip pierced? i wanna get a tattoo
you did yours when you were thirteen.what drugs you taken? smack?
i know shocker used to play warhammer with him hung himself
everyone was in bits one lad ran out of his exam half way through
i keep thinking about cutting again it's worse at night
i'm not going back to the psyche though
'Don't be impulsive, and stay away from the woods.'
fuckin' useless i can't breathe i can't sleep
i'm having the panics dad i can't go to bed
i don't want to stay up better now
i'm knackered yeah i'll brush my tablet & take my teeth LOL
it won't be loud i'll turn it off in a minute
God, two o'clock's early
night dad

Coming off my meds listening to my son tic away

Volume is controlled in units of five
with perfectly timed snorts
during fast forward ad breaks.
Nosebleeds in various scenes,
flicks of the head with lip-smacking
blinks and clacking teeth,
he is a machine of well-practiced tics.

To still his mind he hops and skips
paying attention to his concerns.
In fear of nervous convulsions
he refuses the authority of breakfast.
An involuntary puzzle in class,
he must answer questions of himself.

Instinctive thoughts on repeat require
a parental presence when trying to sleep.
It is in that dark, I see a pyramid scheme
of people, prescriptions, control; intervention
lines rigid as a colony, a map dividing
a soul from a soul. So quietly,
as I prepare for more, I pray for less.

There are charities for all of my unequal parts

'Hope is ravenous like the gulls, and we are being eaten alive.'
Lucia Perillo

Part 1: From the neck down

Low Vitamin D requires 20 mcg per diem; to dissuade
potential crumbling, please handle sunny side up.
Low testosterone is corrected with a rear-view injection
of Nebido, sending the already over-achieving libido
off the scale, causing out-of-your-box protrusions
to rational thought. A collusive beard mentors hairy
areas in how to tuft across once barren land. Stubborn lungs
lay down tools refusing to take part in the must-try-
harder art of breathing. Relief is green & brown, often blue.
A redundant thyroid requires chemical thyroxine,
a.m./p.m. till the end. Cancellation of fight or flight means
I am more dry dock than speedboat with the cortisol.
The pituitary an unreliable narrator, the body's regulator,
hands in its notice causing a hot flush of mental pauses
that soak the body like tears of an actor in between jobs.
The dark overlord of it all – 'friendly-fire' auto-immunity -
is the wandering serial killer of a stuck-in-the-headlights
system of glands, hiding in the bushes of biological ignorance.

Part 2: Thus from the neck up

I fill out CBT's questionnaire in A Minor. I look up words
I don't want to know the meaning of. When the letters
begin spinning like a neurotic nickelodeon I start whistling
anti-clockwise. Weights & measures of the mind convert
to acronyms, making life more difficult to spell. My ears
swim with violins the sound of piano keys aches my bones.
I live to a soundtrack of not keeping up. Crushed up in the arms
of serotonin inhibition I am expected to come away
from a meeting not needing to go back & amplify: *Was I okay?*
At what, I don't know. *Were you puzzled by what I said, or
just that I returned?* I drift in and out like a lost stagehand.
Can I not just tell you I have an aversion to the orders of syntax,
with little interest in staying asleep or being depressed all the time,
only to let my family down from a height I haven't the legs to jump from?

Part 3: Ecology

This body is a computerised diktat of eternal worm-holing
by diabetistic endos, furrowed psyches, & surface cleaning GPs,
who gaze into this body through the parallax lines of a close try.
This body is a stock exchange of wrong turns that burns from
the acid of hope's empty stomach. 'Can you not see it?'

Coming off my meds when you are all asleep

It wasn't made up after all,
those stats percolated
with anecdotes about feeling
alienated from those close
to you. A familiar family anomie
with those right there talking
around the subject, which is you.
I didn't realise you feel
in dreams, did you?

During face, teeth, toilet, coffee,
toast, drive, walk, settle,
I return to wrestle with others'
dimensions, not knowing
whether to analyse or anaesthetise
the who, which, why, where
I fit with the numbers of stories.

So I find it really funny
that for all the drainage
dreaming did to my thoughts
I am so tired I can't help lying
down just two hours later
and going back for more.

Sertraline earworms

Today I am being asked if I know *the muffin man, the muffin man,*
the muffin man, you know, the one who lives down Drury Lane?
I keep telling myself I do, I do, I do know the Muffin Man and if I find
him, I will eat him. But the question is a repeat prescription, sending
me *loop dee loop* in the shop as I fill my bag with the blueberry kind.

My earworm comes in many genres: punk, reggae, dubstep, grime,
I don't mind, but it's pop's incessant water torture of withdrawal.
From Ed Sheeran's *Thinking Out Loud* come guitar loop taps
causing brain zaps that pinball off the walls of my disorder.
When the beat of the SSRI drug slugs away, it leaves a slime of chimes,

setting off lightening bug stage dives into a mosh pit of pharmacology.
Minding my own, a drive-by sample of Britney Spears hits me baby
much much more than one more time. Passing Top Shop, Take That
want me back, they want me back, they really want me back for good.
I want to stick tweezers in my ears & pick out the notes hanging like
funereal earrings.

My wife sings, *oh baby, baby, how was I supposed to know that*
something wasn't right here – I concede that she wasn't, as I try to keep
this swirling wildfire DJ under control. But a moment of OCD
weakness, sees me ask her if she knows *the muffin man, the muffin*
man, the muffin man? To which in turn *she asks, 'the one who lives*
down Drury Lane?' And so *oh baby, baby, it won't stop, it won't stop,*
even when she's not there, even when there is nothing left to hear.

How to keep the little beggars quiet

'Good night, sleep tight
Don't let the bedbugs bite.
But if they do, then take your shoe and
Hit them till they're black and blue.'
Children's Nursery Rhyme

A nipple, a knuckle, a nappy, calpol, sudocream, dummy,
a rattle? (no rattle), chewed up rag they still call *blanky*.
A mobile, a clean arse, a smacked arse, a ten mile push
in the buggy in the middle of the day, driving them
around for ten miles in the middle of the night.

A doll, primary coloured plastic, a train set, an empty box,
CBeebies, a bedtime story. Turning their clock back
four hours, so they think it's only three in the morning.
Carrot sticks, MaccyD chips, Pixar, popcorn, war hammer,
a scooter, a skateboard, dyed hair, a pierced ear, a pierced lip.
An Xbox One, PS4, PC, tablet, smartphone – a power cut.

An orange, a lump of coal, a shilling, money, more money,
a book? (good luck), a letter from the head teacher
you wrote yourself, a leftfield swear word
during dinner, pretending you are sad at the death
of a distant relative they've never heard of,

the death of a grandparent, your own tears,
a finger to your lips, a cane marked palm, a hand raised
above their head, pressed against their mouth,
wrapped around their throat, knives, guns, gangs, drones,
cleansing, dirty water, immolation, in the towns and cities,
villages and provinces, slums and shanties, favelas and camps.
In the homes.   At home.

For Tommy it's all about the music

'*Maggie Thatcher You Can't Match Her*'
is railing on the jukebox for the fifth time
that Sunday night, a time when the women
are at home readying the kids
for future failure and an early night kicking off
their blankets and wetting the bed.

The old Paddies, full of pints & roasts,
lost bets and building site wives, shout
about the *auld whoor* and how she's ruining
the country they came over to build
when they weren't paid enough to build their own.

The young lads are all one-in-ten UB40s,
gabbing about the football, fanny
and who's next for a beating
at pool. Signing away their life
at the social, they can still feel
the cane-lined education across their arse.

Everyone owes everyone else, so all's good,
in this handshake economy – one lad buys
a house off another who's going away for a year
at least, and their days lengthen over outside events
like the grey shadow of a cloak soaked
in the blood of industrial resignation.

Tommy's sat amongst them. Once
a scuffle of calcium, now a jenga of bones
carved in the corner with smoke-gold fingers
and no mind to argue with an empty glass.
He's beaten down by the interventions of time.
Says, he keeps hearing things he never said,
wants someone to call him a psychiatrist
next week. Any day will do, except for the ones

he's dissolved in drink. He's a packed diary.
The lads tell him he's got the experience
but not the qualifications. It's a joke
he doesn't get, but no-one makes the call either.

By the middle of the week Tommy's kitchen
has music dancing off the walls without
a guide rope. A few too many lines, sees him
shaking with uncertain psychosis, and in need
of the padded cell of plant food. So he takes off
to the shop with the fairies, for fags
and skins to roll a coned one. Then sits
in the company of a pigeon decorating
the bench with other white shit from the city's
indulgence. Tommy smiles as the Hail Mary
Jane takes to playing him a soothing tune.

Meanwhile his muscle-in-residence
anabolic neighbour turns up at the empty flat
to tell Tommy he's broken their keep-the-peace agreement
hammered out at three o'clock Monday morning
over empty promises and a full bag of *Super Brew*.
Yer man spots Tommy's powder floured across
the table like the extravagance of an apprentice baker.
He jibs him to the beasts, but not before stealing
a line or three for his own well-tunnelled nostrils.

So now Tommy's bored as a spirit level
in an IKEA showroom. Flat packed
on the lower deck, in a 23 hour lock up.
He suffers his top bunk's bucket list for when
the great outdoors opens once again. This lad
is little more than an 18 year old roll up,
a career choice cock up. A neck tat toe rag,
useful as 90 pence in Poundland, he stinks
of stale digestives. The lad needs crampons
to cling to his delusion, instead of slip up plimsolls
stolen from the pay-us-what-you-got shop.

The lad says he knows the inside of a car
inside out, cackles like a cauldron stirrer, before
showing Tommy his un-fathered hands. For the next
six weeks he is nearly all Tommy will see, laid out
on a diamond wired spring framed mattress,
gabbing on like a trade description act
in a six by ten picture frame for Her Majesty's Pleasure.
Tommy was born in the day, but it wasn't
yesterday. He's got his whole life behind him
and he's losing all feeling toward keeping
another lad safe from a future stretched
out dreaming at the ceiling.

Our Tommy finally gets to see the psych.
They listen to music together with the door shut,
in the prison's excuse for a chapel. Strings and piano
keys echo through the rows of empty chairs;
enough to give Tommy the steadies. And so,
for one hour a week at least, he's free
of all those fellas jabbering away in his head
about Thatcher, the horses, football and the fanny.

Man up man down

'You must go on/I can't go on/I'll go on.'
Samuel Beckett

One only ever got As at school
Two got expelled yet was nobody's fool

Three fell out of his virtual world
Four fell out with his only girl

Five fought too long on foreign sand
Six couldn't keep paying with cash in hand

Seven kept house, kept kids, kept calm
Eight cut one hundred lines on his arm

Nine had a lifelong wife that died
Ten was a man that never cried

Eleven was a man who everyone loved
Twelve was a man who'd had enough

It is fine to rhyme and be poetic
But twelve men down a day is tragic

For most men it goes without saying

after Gil Scott Heron

you will not see ours in HD
3D pixelated w i d e s c r e e n TV
we will not be in any Xtra Large
Big Kahuna burger bundle
box set of YouTube views
Facebook likes nor
Instagrammatical errors

ours will not be televised

ours will not be brought to you
in diagnosable format it will be
no Gif JPEG or HTML
touch-screen experience ours
will not show up in any BAFTA
nominated costume drama
with Stephen Fry and Ruby Wax
we will not man up man down man
turned around by any 0300 24 hour helpline

ours will not go better with
rum & coke smack or toke
we may get fat lose weight
man size have an appetite
for a three course sex drive but

ours will not be televised

there will be no pictures of ours
in tattoo magazines or the cover
of any six-pack of amitriptyline
ours is not the finest smartest
taste the difference range
we are proper essential mate

we will not give Jeremy Kyle
a hard on with daytime DNA claims
in sick-strewn ATOS reports
brought on by aggressive
interview techniques
and signed by some suit
labelled improved behaviour

we will not be seen crying
on your carpet nor begging
on our knees for forgiveness
to dirty the broadsheets
or feed the gullets of
party political red tops

ours will not be televised

it will not be exposed
taken out of context
misquoted or overblown
it will not take kindly to
pop-picking pundits poll of pollsters
nor lay people on the ground
and we will rain on any
homeopathic healers
who try to karaoke away
our pain with an open mic

ours will not be back
after the break there
will be no repeats there
will be no catch up nor
on demand there will be
no highlights no sir because

our depression is LIVE.

Veteran

She stands on the platform in a Royal Ascot Ladies' Day
caramel dress, heels, and new-born tummy. Immaculate,
with her man's jacket in praise around her shoulders

waiting for its master to return from having a slash, but
he is bull-rushing a stranger breaking the bog sink
into nuggets of iceberg marble that tears their shirts

into white flags that only one of them waves, turning
the station into screams as an approaching train
offers an escape from the scene. Sitting with my son, silent,

I patchwork events, slicing images into questions.
Why one man suited for the races, takes to a late running
commuter, that way. His woman calling him

a facking animal, yet clattering after him again. Me,
feeling raw as a debrief when he bouldered past, fragranced
in bleach and sweat. My shame in not going after the cunt,

to hold him down, show him a face with true violence
stuck to it. My son's sense to get me on the train,
then him listening to the call of duty going off in my brain.

A US soldier after Belshazzar's feast

*'God has numbered the days of your kingdom, and brought them
to an end'*
Daniel 5:26

I step through the open gate
for the first time in five years.
Graffiti tags swirl across
the perimeter fence and wall.
It was never this sunny.
On duty it was just hot.
I crack a pack, light up
watching the white stripe
of a jet fighter arc out to sea.
From inside the camp
you could only dream
the ocean was so near.
Escape was a dry mouth
in a jail full of teeth.

I put my folded uniform
on the dust white ground
like a wreath; piss petrol
on it from a small Jerry can.
Torch it with my smoke.
The camouflage jacket takes
its time, smoulders to a flame,
searing through the body
blacking out my name.
I still hear the men now,
a glow of orange suits,
waiting for their empty feast.

A lesson in extreme sports for the untrained soldier

Begin by taking a long march through
his sandstorm hair to see your horizon.
Kayak down the scar on his cheek
where he lay weak for the risk of a cig.
Surf on the crest of his spit, as it hits
the faces of men too scared not to listen.
Boulder along the jut of his chin
then wedge your foot in the cut of his neck.
When secure, abseil down his pecs,
feel the rigor in his sandstone muscles
Tiptoe over his ribs,
but be alert to the marks of fist-shaped crimson
Skateboard across his cobblestone abs,
once moulded out of an ambition to cull
Ollie over his crotch
kept hostage, praying to be let out.
Slide down his thighs that
carried the weight of hours in miles run up hill
Body board his shins,
stubborn as the departing mist-kissed white cliffs
Then lay yourself at his feet, check
the tag on his toe, and hope that it's not you.

Lunchtime

You are one of two empty stomachs
at the table; the other's organs
are laid out like an all-you-can eat feast
for the victor, choice cuts, separated
beyond conception, beyond the sweet
meats of a spoiled war. Your gloves
of UN-blue skies, scoop up globules
of death, slide them back into
the open abdomen. The skin is
a torn curtain, cold under the lights
of tiles and thunder. But this is nothing
to you, who has seen such naked combat,
with its hungry conventions. Draw the flesh
to a close, with surgical indifference,
stale with the monotony of trauma.
Head off to the mess, you've had your fill.

He was a man of many words

Middle-ageing in the mud
he barks at us to run away,
barks again as we return sick
as dogs without sticks. Folding
into question marks, we mist
the grass with mislaid breath.

His words sharpen us upright,
pushing us towards the comfort
of exhaustion. A six-foot training manual
he does this with the humour of a lover
and the fireball throat
of an ex-sergeant major each week.

Where we go back in time,
he goes back to his family,
to his bible, to his pills, to his bed
to his own private sacrifice.

The case of the quiet caretaker

Our subject takes a flower without consequence
from a passing garden, glad-hands it to Mister
Broad Suit from a number up the street who keys
his pay-grade beamer, returning a plain-clothes
smile, before driving away to his day. Every other

morning, our subject takes over from a forty-five
degree outstretched parent pushing a buggy-covered
child on the way to its daily play. A swirl
of Ice-lolly wrappers wait impatiently for him
by a bin – his pockets are deep come collection day.

When the woman next door-but-three leaves
the house of a Monday morning, he cleans
her windows, top & bottom/back & front
wishing he could do them from the inside.
It takes at least a week to clean his street's

snow-covered drives inside the banquet
of a bright empty night. Out driving, he stops
to give people the lift he believes they expect
from him. One regular accepter with no fixtures
or fittings always takes to the car's musical

taste. Turns it too loudly for anybody's liking,
as he taps the dash in haste of threadbare times.
No complaint is ever made nor money taken.
Our subject fills his tank when still three quarters
full. Holds his breath, when watching people go

under at the pool. He treats everyone with
alphabetical respect. Stops introducing himself
only after he has met the person six times. He may
know what everyone needs. Such anonymous devotion
takes time. You will observe our subject forever

looking over his shoulder; not to see if he is being followed,
but to see if he is getting in nature's way.

Colluding with the enemy

St Albans 1918

'Pure gold that bar' is how he described it soon after
the Great War. I'd not tasted the likes. Truth be told,
made me feel a little sick, bitter and dark like new-born coal.

But shared with 'the enemy' in Dad's field, flavour
felt like a well-kept secret, blurring visions of men and war,
of who was who. The man liked it here that was for sure.

'Good as any German kind,' he said, as he savoured
a chunk with a wink. They sent him back when the flags
came down. Took another war before I got a small bag

of souvenirs from Germany, with twelve bars of chocolate
inside, wrapped in gold, like a roll of sovereigns in my pocket.

Our lost history

for Maya

In Farringdon's once fertile valley we rest our ears
on the road. Marking our cheeks with a drain plate's name
we listen to the hollow brook of a lost river that roars

defiant beneath our chests. Strata of difference are drawn
from the maps we walk across; the woodblock detail of Agas,
the spectrum of poverty in Booth's yellow *upper classes*, down

to blackened *vicious semi-criminals*, markers of wealth not worth.
The remains of Romans still earth the traffic, layered by Christian
and pagan burials – of Huguenots, Italians, Jews and the new; sewn,

stitched, wound up and praised. We stroll through the vineyards
of Norman Holborn, rising up herbal hill to redden our bare feet
with saffron. Back down from Windmills, to Turnmills, to Hell,

there are saints amongst the Knights of St John, angels even,
with weavers' in their lofts rising to the light, clockmakers,
brewers reviving their craft, to the bleeding heart of Hatton

who left his gardens to the jewellers. We take the track back
where dirt was turned to gold and see the Clerk's Well encased
in silence. There, where horses once took water, rests the fountain

once preserved with flowers. We carry their smell to the Betsey,
drink wine from the House, forgetting where our past first met.

Meat down the Cally

His granddad was famous, you know.
A train driver, with his very own
cigarette card. People used to bow
to him, as he walked down the Cally Road.

He was a sort of God to them so he was.
It was his trains delivered the cows.
Thousands of 'em ran up the Cally to slaughter;
clopping, snorting and stinking up the street.

Steam rising off them in the cold morning.
Mothers brought their kids, all wrapped up,
to breathe the cattle's steamy sweat,
to quieten the little 'uns whooping cough.

Dirty old men sought out the calves,
who were hungry for their mother's teat.
He didn't take to the trains; it was the knife
for him, aged fifteen. Five in the morning

in the White Hart, necking pints before
the shift's start. Never went to work
sober. Only thing he ever cut was the cattle.
Take a look at his hands. No knife

of his made those marks.You see all
those flats now, row after row
they were just one big slaughterhouse
back then. If people knew how many cattle

were killed there, I don't think
they'd live there, I don't think they could.
When the cattle were all gone, he went
to Much Hadham. But only found

a load of old peace and quiet there.
So he made it back to the Cally, to hear
the ambulances, fire engines and trains.
That keep him awake. That keep him sane.

This isn't a party, my friend

Okay, the heavy stuff first, a front load
24 pack of lager, *beep*, whisky, *beep*, vodka,
beep, and four bottles of red, tap, tap, *beep*.
Bag of spuds, *beep*, carrots, *beep*, onions, *beep*,
bread and four pints full fat milk, *beep beep*,
you've got your staples cracked.

One arse-sized steak, *beep*, one steroid chicken, *beep*.
bacon, sausage, and eggs, *beep*, *beep*, *beep*.
Crisps, crackers, nuts, multi-bag of cheesy Wotsits, four *beeps*,
a Victoria sponge cake, *beep*, chocolate eclairs, *beep*,
and your Bourbons and Garibaldi's, *beep*, *beep*.
Vive la revolution! What no veg? What no veg? Oh,
a small bag of frozen peas, *beep*, Black Forest Gateaux,
Meat Feast Pizza, Chicken Dippers, and 36 Fish Fingers,
beep, *beep*, *beep*, *beep*.

48 rolls of toilet paper, *beep*, air freshener, *beep*.
Is that all love? Oh, sorry, I didn't see the Gaviscon,
Rennie, Alka Selzter. Milk of Magnesia.*beep diddly beep,
to infinity and beyond*! Tap, tap, tap, that all comes to
a BP of 160 over 110, 120 for your BPM, plus ten for your lipids,
and a 50 BMI that makes you go, *Beep, Beep, Beep, Beep,
Beeeeeeep*!

Testosterone injection

Passing a line of traffic, with a dull ache in my right buttock, dressed to express a deep need to be anonymous, I hear the purse of a kiss from some paint-speckled cock of a bloke out the window of his mate's white van. I turn, wink as in a tic, smile, walk on. The dough balls double a laugh behind me. I try to resort to dormant but can only compare notes. Does he not see, I too once pulled an all-nighter, spilling into a Sunday morning football changing room full of towel-slapped arses with shrivelled cocks like a nest of baby birds, topped off with jokes about your mum's appetite for young men? Does he not see, I've drank with mortar mix pay packet fingers, knees crushed by concrete, soft as an open-all-hours wound. Does he not see I was an end-of-the-week bookies' wet dream, waging till my pockets were as vacant as my head. Does he not see, I could get a crap tattoo from a mate with the misspelled name of an old flame still burning up my past? Does he not see, I could harvest a generation of skinny-chinned kids from pebble-dashed inner-city landscapes. Does he not see, I could give him a proper kiss, one I learned from my Dad and he's from Glasgow. No? Then take this poem as a handshake, for how else can a real man see himself for what he really is?

Chatting up the barmaid

I spotted a set of spoons in Oxfam's window
this morning, only £9.99 they were, probably
worth a fortune no doubt. Be a good starter kit
for those wanting to make a better life
for themselves. I could imagine a set of my own,
or some such silver – sat next to Uncle Arthur
above the fireplace in my bedsit. Cheaper than
the tattoos he collected at sea, lot less painful
as well I reckon, funny bugger. Must be
great having like-minded collectors to share
your life with; who don't give a shit about
the 'what you do that for?' way of thinking.
I used to collect tadpoles as a kid. Kept them
in a bucket, until my mum lifted up the lid
to find a box of frogs, jumping up her best
Friday night skirt. I collect Nazi memorabilia
now. Medals mainly, some knives, a helmet.
I'm on the lookout for the full uniform,
the Wehrmacht, not the SS kind – the bastards.
How about you sweetheart? What treasures
you got hidden away behind the bar?

We are none of us Sisyphus

A man shames us, running with hot coal feet,
challenging Newton on the slope of Hellvelyn.
Our sunken chests are thankful for the rest,
to reassess our perspective. We try to laugh

our way up the mountain, knowing it will laugh
right back with wind, sleet and millennia.
Achievements take many dimensions but
for middle-aged men of delusion, vertical is king.

The white spine of Striding Edge mocks
our avoidance, as we huddle at the summit
of puzzled stones and pass round a spliff.
I look down to see my sons at home locked away

in the present, then my parents in the stillness
of their fading. As we descend upon a judder
of jellied thighs, I realise it was stupid to think
I could carry the whole damn mountain back with me.

A classical 4-4-2 formation

a decimal for Jo Bell

In our freedom of a half-time feed, no food is out of bounds.
Pies from heaven, hot beef tea, burnt burgers in dry batches
we steal our fill of trans-fat foundations for after-hour rounds.
Up a stand of plastic thrones, across a cattle of anxious faces,

we find our place with the Gods. On the pitch twenty-two puppets,
steam in the floodlit chill, stringing their legs along, as they wait
for the ref. A rippling sound chases itself from the speakers.
'Is that a harp?' 'It is you know'. Up on the screen is the penguin

in charge, plucking the fuck out of the old country's golden ear,
our herald, we now only see on the glass of a cold black weeping beer.

Ezekiel's burden

In the slice and dice of a Sunday aftermath,
layers of roast lamb lie beached on a plate
resting in the steam along with a playground
of minted peas, carrots, tokens of broccoli.
Yorkshires filled with ponds of gravy, duck
fat roast potatoes, gold as the wedding ring
in his pocket. Piled high in the loading bay,
waits the comfort of homemade bread –
baked over the heat of his own waste.

Like all meals – fish & chips first thing,
deep-fried pie up the match, full English
of a weekend, curry after the pub,

he eats them as a high-rise sandwich
clenched in horizontal prayer to a shiny chin.
Never with butter, never needs to lick
the plate. Full of bread he will rise, dry-eyed,
zip his bomber jacket right up tight against
a walnut Adam's apple, and head out.
This watchman will then take the time
to chat down lads who still fill their faces
with the pure shit of their own voracity.

It's not a matter of life and death, but still

Saturday morning is a flurry of flailing sons with toe-poke attitudes
in front of goal, as their dads redraw mythical glories from shivering

side-lines. The afternoon is a three o'clock corrugated terrace, filled
with expectations of close up failure and 'there's always mid-week'.

Back home after the pub for a night-time recount to a daytime widow,
foil fat fodder takeaway in front of *Match of the Day* and lost hope

of a blow job explosion that will end with a TV tan sleeping on
a belly full of everything. Sunday is veterans' morning, where sons

are forced to watch dads in whale-shaped kits & blindfolded joints
kicking at memories above a shuddering earth. A ball over the top

sees one dad fall back, on a well-cushioned crack. In a heart-stopping
moment a son with hand-me-down mimicry shouts, '*Get up Dad,*

he hardly touched you', laughing with his mates, whose own dads
gather round the stricken fella with bowed heads and forgotten lines.

Bored to death

At certain times of the day, on uncertain days,
he makes play of the sunlight; spotlights his ruined

room from a gold can. Shimmering the late rays
with yellowing smoke. Other times off his watch, a ruined

face, a tale of scratched streaks against fading flock
walls; a pattern not noticed before, blaming a ruined

eyesight for blurring time. He uses this boredom
to block the bone soaked ritual of precocious ruin,

to drift away after visits from one-time strugglers
now beyond hearing. Close to their own ruin,

they married an escape in unexpected numbers.
He now travels in time, a recall joy ride of past ruins

never taking care to trace a line that arrives
in a room staging the finale of his inevitable ruin.

If you don't go to theirs, they won't go to yours

for Timmy

A hearse, a hymn, whisky breath men, carry him in
amidst a chorus of incense. A rasping Rosary
from a bidden patriarch, echoes with those way past
the five decades of our friend, the first of us to go.

We are all there, backs broken by the practice
of prayer, still steeped in the dim rituals of service.
A Roman century of suits guards the aisles for the Priest.
I have never heard such silence amongst them. After,

at ties off, jackets hug chairs, fists clench pints, smiles
stretch cheeks. I look around at the celebrants of a life
well-worn. A shadow of them comes into view. Histories
panel the club like a final roll call of dislocated soldiers.

I leave before old stories are lost to the drink, but wonder,
if I last, could I come back to this, a hundred times more?

In the Words of St Peter

Once through the gates, Tommy found a place in the corner where
he chips away at his eggshell skin. No longer the lumpen-hump
of a man, he's having a bit of nip and tuck done later, to take out
the vertebrae of drugs that line his spine, a ready-made
jet pack from a previous life. Fast as fuck he'd be back before
he left, which makes total sense if you don't think about it.

His wife had a cemetery of laughter streaming out
her rowing boat when he passed; his two kids rotting
on the kerb like leftovers from a Saturday night can't
Save the Children take-out, missing body parts of a broken
fortune cookie. Tommy knew not to swallow the shit floating
over fields of police cells, pulpits, & out-of-hours services.

Forever a skeleton key of opportunity, an emergency weekend
timetable, a replacement busted flush, forever fiddling
with the metre of infinity. Tommy was built from his own rock
as were many like him who turn up in this place, eyeless
from the drink, their withered work-length arms,
a habit of hammers still swinging away in their darkness.

Is it writing or is it typing?

Published by Fuck-Knows-Who Press, this poet's collection is described as an epic tome of sixteen and three quarter short poems about the trials and defibrillations at his allotment. On reading however, it hardly stretches to the static life of a neglected window box.

We are told, *'there are 247 end rhymes and 311 internal rhymes which surpass the joint record held by Wendy Cope & Pam Ayres.'* (It fails to mention however, that these numbers fall well short of any found in one of those rapping person's bars).

Instances of assonance pass as nonsense with all the sass of an un-wiped ass. There is an allusive alliance of alliteration, where the reader's alleviation, is merely allegorical. The metres of metre bounce along the track like a stressed/unstressed Usain Bolt in a straightjacket.

I was particularly unsympathetic to the epidemic of abstract nouns that made me feel disappointed, angry, and had me reaching for an out-of-date bottle of milk of amnesia. The similes fail in their claim to be *'paradoxical metaphors symbolic of a dystopic utopian garden'*; they are more like a rocking high/horse of like-minded people dancing in a blender.

The preponderant sonnets are meant to be neo-Petrarchan, but are in fact, faux Don Paterson (I hear Paterson intends to sue). The poet's misguided penchant for the surreal appears in poems that are orange with concrete feathers that fly over a horse, painting a watch found in the cavity of his sprinkler system's sexuality.

Overall the form is erratic and unreflective of any of the poems' intent to show the wildness of his allotment/window box when a westerly wind blows ashes from the cemetery across the road. The free verse poems should be locked up. If stanzas are rooms, then our poet is a slum landlord.

Quotidian themes of love, loss, death, and grief, are all covered in a single haiku, here it is in all its 'glory':

I live with what death
leaves: love, loss, a compost of
pesticidal grief.

Like much poetry the book is bereft of rage; where is the anger at the 2% increase in allotment fees, or the hatred towards fellow allotmenters at their merciless mockery of his courgettes that look like a Jolly Green John Thomas in need of Viagra?

The blurb on the back cover from the poet's estranged mother, says that to truly appreciate her son's work the reader should tear out all of the pages and post each one through their neighbours' doors just to confirm their loathing of poetry.

The poems are nowhere near finished, and should certainly be abandoned. All in all, it is a terrible collection, and I loved it to death.

How to avoid poetry

Don't get sent down. Don't stand on picket lines.
Don't listen to Beyoncé's *Lemonade.*
Keep away from aftermaths. Don't teach.
Don't have children, don't have children
that teach. Keep off that Internet. Don't
watch regal celebrations, war centenaries,
or Presidential inaugurations. Good luck
with christenings, weddings & funerals.
Keep your head down on the underground,
doctor's or hipster cafés. Avoid canal boats,
gardens, community centres & play areas
as well as newsagents' notice boards.

When a friend tells you they've started reading poetry,
give them a look as if God was a gasman & make your excuses.

Don't live next door to someone who's home in the day
but doesn't own a telly. Avoid four-minute slots on Channel 4,
arts programmes on BBC 2 or 4, or nature programmes
presented by a middle-aged psycho-geographic poet with an
earring.

Don't turn on the FA Cup Final until kick-off. Don't go
upstairs in a pub on a weekday. Don't walk
to the back of a bookshop or library. Don't go
to the cinema, local council cultural festivals,
or European Cities of Culture (you hear me Coventry).

Don't stay at home sitting in the dark too long
as you might weaken; if you're not gaining strength
from philosophy, self-help books, or Dave
behind the bar, drop some acid & eat
a box-set of Jennifer Aniston films.

Please keep this list to hand in order to avoid
this esoteric & little loved pursuit.
Don't say you haven't been warned.
Goodbye and thank you for reading.

Acknowledgements

Thanks are due to the editors of the following publications where early versions of some of these poems were first published: *Culture Matters, Campaign Against Living Miserably (CALM), Domestic Cherry, Eye Flash, Poetry For Every Year Project, the Fat Damsel, HappenStance, the High Window, Ink Sweat & Tears, The Interpreter's House, MIND anthology, the Morning Star, New Left Project, Prole, Queen Mobs Teahouse, the Rialto, South Bank Poetry, Under the Radar* and *Vanguard Editions*.

To Brian Harrison who dared me to choose the poetry module for our Masters; it was led by Malika Booker and poetry became everything. To Jo Bell for her encouragement, humour and giving me the antidote to abstract nouns. To Malika's Poetry Kitchen crew, especially Captain Jill Abram. To those who have helped and influenced me on the way: Mona Arshi, Rishi Dastidar, Inua Ellams, Melissa Lee-Houghton, Fran Lock, Kim Moore, Pascale Petit, Clare Pollard, Richard Skinner, Anna Robinson, Julia Webb, and Tim Wells. I am particularly grateful to Jane Commane who read an earlier draft of this collection. To the Arts Council for funding the research and writing.

Thanks to my children and family for giving me much of the raw material; and my wife Maya, who although still doesn't read poetry, listens to it because I read it to her most days. And finally, for Cov!